EXPLORERS

John C.
Frémont

Kristin Petrie

ABDO
Publishing Company

visit us at
www.abdopub.com

Published by ABDO Publishing Company, 4940 Viking Drive, Edina, Minnesota 55435. Copyright © 2004 by Abdo Consulting Group, Inc. International copyrights reserved in all countries. No part of this book may be reproduced in any form without written permission from the publisher.

Printed in the United States.

Cover Photos: Corbis
Interior Photos: Corbis pp. 5, 7, 9, 10, 11, 13, 16, 17, 21, 23, 24, 27, 29; Library of Congress p. 25; North Wind pp. 15, 22, 26

Series Coordinator: Stephanie Hedlund
Editors: Kate A. Conley, Kristin Van Cleaf
Art Direction & Cover Design: Neil Klinepier
Interior Design & Maps: Dave Bullen

Library of Congress Cataloging-in-Publication Data

Petrie, Kristin, 1970-
    John C. Frémont / Kristin Petrie.
       p. cm. -- (Explorers)
    Includes index.
    Summary: A biography of the nineteenth-century soldier, politician, and explorer whose many expeditions helped open up the American West to settlers.
    ISBN 1-59197-602-2
    1. Frâmont, John Charles, 1813-1890--Juvenile literature. 2. Explorers--West (U.S.)--Biography--Juvenile literature. 3. Explorers--United States--Biography--Juvenile literature. 4. Presidential candidates--United States--Biography--Juvenile literature. 5. Generals--United States--Biography--Juvenile literature. 6. West (U.S.)--Discovery and exploration--Juvenile literature. [1. Frâmont, John Charles, 1813-1890. 2. Explorers. 3. West (U.S.)--Discovery and exploration.] I. Title.

E415.9.F8P48 2004
973.6'092--dc22
    [B]   2003066520

Contents

John C. Frémont

In the early 1800s, the land we know as the United States was mostly wilderness. Many people believed the land west of the Mississippi River was barren. In fact, much of the continent was called the Great American Desert. John C. Frémont proved these theories wrong.

Frémont mapped much of the land between the Rocky Mountains and the Pacific Ocean. His descriptions painted a new picture of the West for early Americans.

John C. Frémont became known as the Pathmarker. This American was an explorer, military man, and politician. His work helped the nation stretch from the Atlantic Ocean to the Pacific.

1451
Christopher Columbus born

1485
Hernán Cortés born

1450
John Cabot born

1460
Vasco da Gama born

1491
Jacques Cartier born

John C. Frémont

1492
Columbus's first voyage west for Spain

1496
Cabot's first voyage for England

1493
Columbus's second voyage, attempted to colonize Hispaniola

John's Childhood

John C. Frémont was the first child of Mrs. Anne Pryor and Jean Charles Frémon. Anne and Jean were in love. However, this caused much **controversy** during their years together.

In 1796, Anne Whiting had married Major John Pryor. The marriage had been arranged to secure Anne's family wealth. The young woman was unhappy in her marriage to a much older man. But then in 1810, Anne fell in love with a Frenchman named Jean Charles Frémon.

Anne and Jean ran away together and settled in Savannah, Georgia. On January 21, 1813, the couple had a son named John Charles Frémon. They soon had another son and a daughter. However, little is known about John's **siblings**.

1497
Cabot's second voyage, discovered the Grand Banks; da Gama was first to sail around Africa to India

1496 or 1497
Hernando de Soto born

1498
Cabot's third voyage, may have died; Columbus's third voyage

Around 1814, Major Pryor died. So, Jean and Anne married. When Jean died in 1818, the widow and her children moved to Charleston, South Carolina. Anne supported the family by running a boardinghouse. She then added a *t* to their last name, making it Frémont.

Savannah, Georgia

1502
Columbus's fourth voyage; da Gama's second voyage

1506
Columbus died

1504
Cortés sailed to the West Indies

School Years

The Frémonts were poor. However, John was bright, and he impressed many people. The first was a lawyer named John Mitchell.

Mitchell hired 13-year-old John to be a clerk in his law office. John's work was **accurate** and complete. Mitchell thought the boy could go far. So, he decided to pay for John's preparatory schooling.

At first, John excelled in school. He had a talent for science and languages. When John was 16, he began studying at the College of Charleston. By the time he was 18, however, John had fallen behind in his studies and become unruly. He was asked to leave the college before he could graduate.

Fortunately, a man named Joel Poinsett was impressed with John. Poinsett found John a job teaching math aboard the USS *Natchez*. He was on the ship when it toured the coast of South America in 1833.

1511
Cortés helped take over Cuba

1510
Francisco Vásquez de Coronado born

1514
De Soto went to the New World

Would You?

Would you help out a young man like John C. Frémont? Why do you think John Mitchell and Joel Poinsett did?

In 1831, John C. Frémont left the College of Charleston.

The Corps

In 1835, John began working for the U.S. Topographical Corps. This was the army's land **surveying** division. John helped plan a railroad route from North Carolina to Ohio. During this assignment, he developed a passion for the outdoors.

Senator Thomas Benton

John was selected for more surveying jobs with the corps. In 1838, he surveyed the upper Mississippi and Missouri rivers with Jean-Nicolas Nicollet. Nicollet trained John in mapmaking and taught him how to identify plants and rocks.

John's successful surveys helped him become a second lieutenant in the corps. About this time,

1524
Da Gama's third voyage, died in Cochin, India

1519–1521
Cortés conquered the Aztec Empire and claimed Mexico for Spain

1532
De Soto helped attack the Inca Empire

Missouri's senator Thomas Benton wanted the U.S. government to promote settlement in the West. Good maps were needed to guide settlers. So, John began to work closely with Senator Benton.

In 1840, John and the senator's young daughter, Jessie Benton, fell in love. The following year they married. Through the years, John and Jessie had three sons and two daughters. However, two of the children died when they were young.

Jessie Benton married John C. Frémont in 1841.

Surveying

Senator Benton helped Frémont get **surveying** jobs in the following years. In 1842, Frémont began his first independent survey. Its goal was to map the route to South Pass, which is a **plateau** in the Rocky Mountains.

With amazing luck, Frémont met frontiersman Kit Carson near the beginning of his assignment. Carson guided Frémont's expedition through the Rockies. He would later be a guide for many of Frémont's missions.

Frémont mapped the South Pass. Then, the men explored the Wind River Range in southern Wyoming. There, Frémont climbed the highest mountain he could find. Soon after he placed an American flag at the top, the group headed home.

Frémont's second independent expedition began in 1843. It traveled northwest from Missouri, across the Rockies, and into Oregon. This route would become known as the

1534
Cartier's first voyage for France

1539–1542
De Soto explored La Florida

1533
De Soto helped take over Cuzco

1535
Cartier's second voyage

Oregon Trail. From there, Frémont and his group turned south and explored Nevada and California.

Frémont returned to Missouri in August 1844. His report to **Congress** included maps, sketches, and useful advice. Thousands of pioneers would use the report when they headed west.

The mountain Frémont climbed was later named Fremont Peak.

The Mexican War

In 1845, Frémont and 60 men explored the Great Basin. It is a large desert region in the western United States. From there, they explored the Pacific Coast. At that time, the area was governed by Mexico.

Frémont and his men carried guns and **ammunition** for protection. However, their guns led the Mexican government to believe the explorers planned to take over the land. So, Frémont was asked to leave. Instead, Frémont built a fort.

In 1845, the United States added Texas to its land. The U.S. and Mexican governments disagreed about the correct border of Texas. This argument led to the Mexican War in 1846. Frémont's job then changed from explorer to soldier. Now, his mission was to help the United States gain California.

For six months, the Americans and Mexicans fought for control over California. In January 1847, the fighting ended. California was added to the United States.

1541
Cartier's third voyage, attempted to colonize Canada; Cortés volunteered to fight against Algiers

1540
Coronado set out to find the Seven Cities of Cíbola; Francis Drake born

Would you think Frémont's group was trying to take over the area? Why would the Mexican government think they were?

Frémont used horses to travel across rough terrain such as the Great Basin and the Pacific Coast.

1547
Cortés died

1557
Cartier died

1542
Coronado returned to New Spain; de Soto died

1554
Coronado died

1566
Drake's first voyage to the New World

Court-Martial

On January 16, 1847, U.S. Navy commodore Robert F. Stockton made Frémont California's governor. But, U.S. Army general Stephen Watts Kearny wanted this position for himself. Kearny claimed he had the highest rank and appointed himself governor.

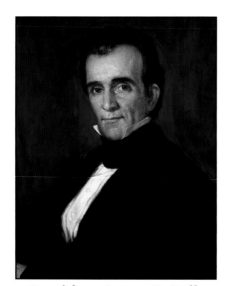

President James K. Polk

Frémont didn't know whose orders to follow. He decided to side with Stockton and continued governing the region. In March 1847, President James K. Polk declared Kearny governor of California. Frémont was released from his position.

Kearny ordered Frémont to return east. He then arrested Frémont for **insubordination**. Frémont was **court-martialed** and found guilty of **mutiny**. He was dismissed from the army.

1567
Drake's second voyage

1577
Drake began a worldwide voyage, was first Englishman to sail the Pacific Ocean

1570 and 1572
Drake terrorized the Spanish in the New World

However, President Polk believed Frémont was not guilty of **mutiny**. He overruled the dismissal, allowing Frémont to remain in the army. But by this time, Frémont was disgusted. He quit the army and turned to a life in the West.

Frémont continued exploring and mapping the West after his court-martial.

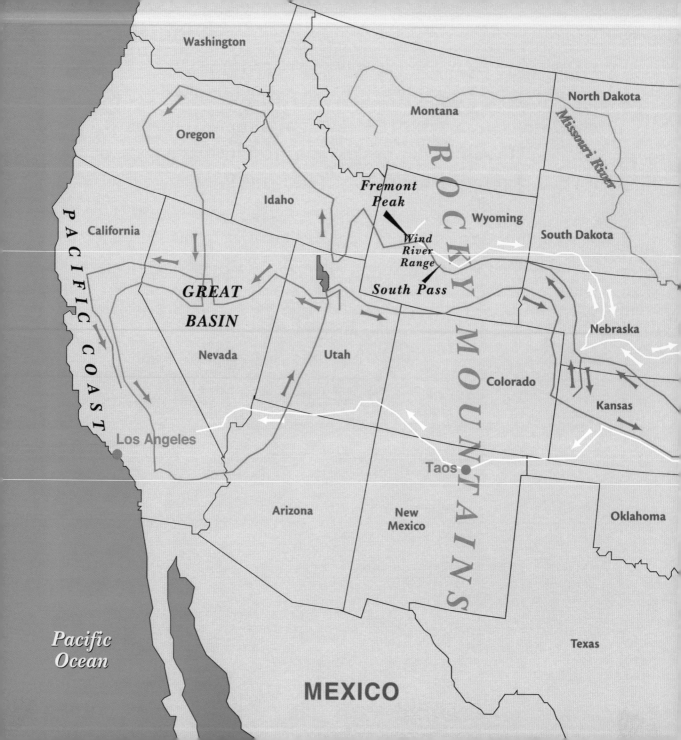

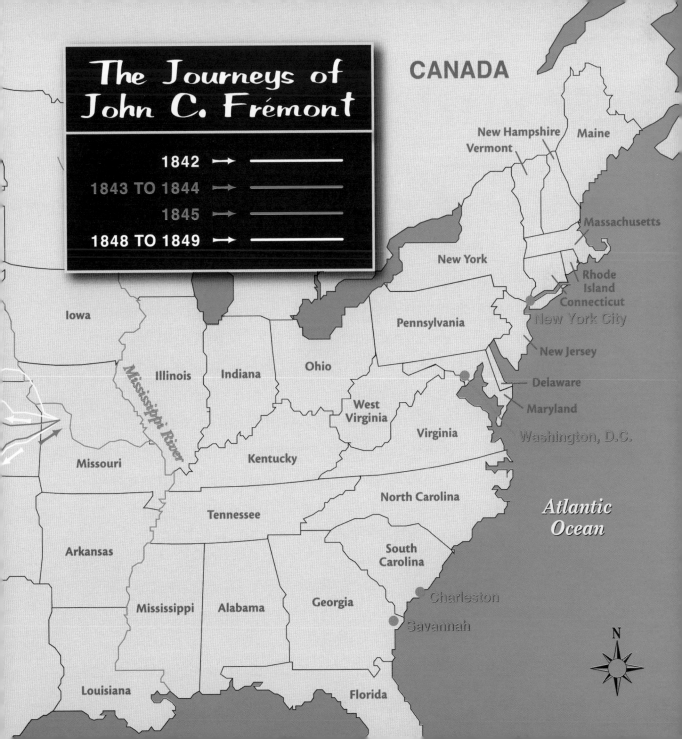

The Journeys of John C. Frémont

1842 →	
1843 TO 1844 →	
1845 →	
1848 TO 1849 →	

CANADA

New Hampshire · Maine

Vermont

Massachusetts

New York

Rhode Island

Connecticut

New York City

Pennsylvania

New Jersey

Delaware

Maryland

Washington, D.C.

Iowa

Illinois

Indiana

Ohio

West Virginia

Virginia

Mississippi River

Missouri

Kentucky

North Carolina

Tennessee

Atlantic Ocean

Arkansas

South Carolina

Charleston

Mississippi

Alabama

Georgia

Savannah

Louisiana

Florida

N

A Cold Mission

After leaving the army, Frémont began his fourth expedition. Its goal was to find a suitable railroad route from Missouri to California. This route had to be passable at any time of year, including winter.

Frémont reached the Rockies in October 1848. Experienced mountain men warned him not to try crossing the region in the winter. Nevertheless, Frémont and 33 men continued on. By December, many of Frémont's men were starving and frostbitten. In the end, 11 men died.

In January 1849, Frémont and the remaining men reached Taos, New Mexico. The expedition had been a bust. No suitable railway routes had been found through the Rocky Mountains. Frémont gave up his search. He traveled to California where his family waited for him.

1588
Drake helped England win the Battle of Gravelines against Spain's Invincible Armada

1581
Drake knighted by Queen Elizabeth I

1596
Drake died

Would You?

Would you listen to the mountain men and stop the mission? Why was it important to find a railway route that would work during all seasons?

Frémont attempted to find the best route across the Rocky Mountains on several different expeditions.

1728
James Cook born

1765
Boone journeyed to Florida

1768
Cook sailed for Tahiti

1734
Daniel Boone born

1767
Boone explored Kentucky

In Politics

On the way to California, Frémont heard good news. Gold had been discovered on his land there! The Frémonts were soon wealthy from their gold mines.

Frémont took on a new role in California. In September 1850, he was elected as one of the new state's first two senators. With his newfound power, Frémont took a bold stand against slavery. Because of this, he lost his position in March 1851.

Five years later, Frémont was back in politics. The **Democratic** Party asked him to run for president. He turned down this opportunity because the Democrats were in favor of slavery.

Miners pan for gold during the California Gold Rush of 1849.

However, the newly formed **Republican** Party opposed slavery. Its members believed John C. Frémont was the perfect man to represent their views. So, Frémont became their first presidential candidate in the 1856 election. In the end, the **Democratic** opponent, James Buchanan, won the election.

Frémont's presidential campaign ribbon from 1856

1778
Cook became the first European to record Hawaiian Islands; Boone captured by Shawnee

1775
Boone cut the Wilderness Road from Virginia to Kentucky

1779
Cook died

Civil War

In 1861, the **Civil War** broke out. President Abraham Lincoln appointed Frémont to a rank of major general in the **Union** army. He was put in charge of the western department, based in Missouri.

One of the central issues of the Civil War was slavery. This issue, along with others, led the **Confederate** states to leave the Union. In August 1861, Frémont used his new authority to proclaim freedom for slaves in Missouri.

Abraham Lincoln

President Lincoln feared that many Southern Union states would join Confederate forces if slavery were illegal. So, he ordered Frémont to modify his proclamation. When Frémont refused, he was relieved of his position.

1813
John C. Frémont born

1842
Frémont's first independent surveying mission

1820
Boone died

Many of Frémont's supporters thought he was wrongly dismissed. So, Lincoln gave him a second chance. In 1862, Frémont was made commander of the **Union**'s mountain department in Virginia.

The Union army's troops were poorly fed and clothed. Frémont's troops were nearly starving and were no match for the **Confederate** army. So, Lincoln joined Frémont's troops with two other regiments.

President Lincoln wrote this letter asking Frémont to change his 1861 proclamation.

Later Years

Frémont was unwilling to work under the combined regiments' new commander. He soon requested a new position. He waited a year for another assignment. When no orders were given, he resigned from the army for good.

Finished with the armed forces, Frémont became interested in business. He moved his family to New York City. Frémont put his money into railroad construction and lived happily for a short time.

John C. Frémont

Unfortunately, the good life had ended by 1864. His partners in California had cheated him, and his gold mines were running dry. The railroad business was suffering, too. The Frémonts were forced to sell their estates in California and New York.

1856
Frémont ran for president of the United States but lost

1845-1846
Frémont explored the Great Basin and the Pacific Coast, fought in the Mexican War

1890
Frémont died

By 1872, the Frémonts were broke. During this time, Jessie wrote articles to earn money. Then from 1878 to 1883, Frémont served as governor of the Arizona Territory. After writing his **memoirs** in 1887, the Frémonts retired in Los Angeles.

Three years later, the army provided Frémont with a **pension**. John C. Frémont died a few months later on July 13, 1890. He was visiting New York at the time. The Frémonts were so poor, Jessie could not afford to travel to her husband's funeral. Jessie Benton Frémont died in 1902.

New York City in the 1860s

1910
Jacques Cousteau born

1951
Cousteau's first expedition in the Red Sea

1942
Cousteau and Gagnan developed the Aqua-Lung for diving

The Legacy

John C. Frémont accomplished much in his life. He was a bright young man and student. He was a teacher and **surveyor**. He was an explorer and man of the wilderness.

Frémont was also a leader and businessman. He boldly entered the world of politics. He served as a senator and a governor. He even attempted to become the president.

The Pathmarker led the way for westward expansion of the United States. John C. Frémont's maps and descriptions were used by thousands of settlers. With his help, the United States now stretches from the Atlantic Ocean to the Pacific.

Opposite page: **John C. Frémont was respected for his work mapping the American frontier.**

Would you want to have adventures such as those of John C. Frémont? What do you think was his greatest achievement?

Glossary

accurate - free of errors.

ammunition - bullets, shells, and other items used in firearms.

civil war - a war between groups in the same country. The United States of America and the Confederate States of America fought a civil war from 1861 to 1865.

Confederacy - the states that left the Union between 1860 and 1861.

Congress - the lawmaking body of the United States. It is made up of the Senate and the House of Representatives. It meets in Washington, D.C.

controversy - discussion between groups with strongly different views.

court-martial - a trial by a military court for members of the armed forces.

Democrat - a member of the Democratic political party. Democrats supported farmers and landowners.

insubordination - refusal to obey a superior, especially in the military.

memoir - a written account of a person's experiences.

mutiny - open rebellion against lawful authority, especially by sailors or soldiers against their officers.

pension - money for people to live on after they retire.

plateau - a raised area of flat land.

Republican - a member of the Republican political party. During the Civil War, Republicans were liberal and against slavery.

sibling - a brother or sister.

survey - to measure a piece of land to determine its shape, area, and boundaries.

Union - the states that remained in the United States during the Civil War.

John Cabot *Christopher Columbus* *Francisco Vásquez de Coronado*

Daniel Boone *Jacques Cartier* *James Cook*

Saying It

James Buchanan - JAYMZ byoo-KAN-uhn
Jean-Nicolas Nicollet - zhahn-nee-kaw-lah nee-kaw-leh
Joel Poinsett - JOH-uhl POYN-seht
memoir - MEHM-wahr
proclamation - prah-kluh-MAY-shuhn
Taos - TOUS

Web Sites

To learn more about John C. Frémont, visit ABDO Publishing Company on the World Wide Web at **www.abdopub.com**. Web sites about John C. Frémont are featured on our Book Links page. These links are routinely monitored and updated to provide the most current information available.

Index